M.E Giguere

New from Amazon Best Selling Author

THis Is My

Confession

M.E Giguere

Trient Press

TRIENTREPRENEUR

ISSUE 10

JUNE AUTHOR TIPS

Tips for authors on Instagram.

- Use Hashtags Strategically
- Run Giveaways
- Stick to the 80/20 Rule
- Engage Engage Engage
- Make Opportunities
- Post Often
- Ask Questions
- Don't Buy Followers
- Sponsor a Post
- Study and Experiment

NEW RELEASES

SELF HELP & MOTIVATION

From personal developement to business advice we have you covered.

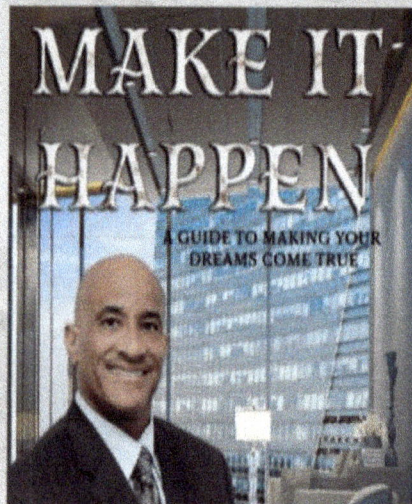

Make It Happen
by debut author Miguel Sanchez

WORKBOOKS

Are You Happy & Are You Happy a Guid to Everyday Happiness

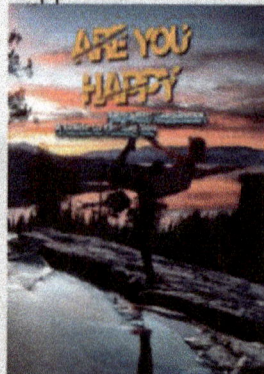

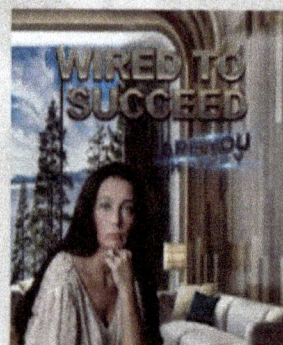

Are you Happy:
Wired for Success

by: M.L.Ruscsak

Cyber Security

Cyber Threats of Today

M.L.Ruscsak

Let me start by saying I am not in cyber security by trade. and I can hear the moans and groans across the computer screen or even through the pages of this magazine. If I'm not in cyber security why am I here to discuss the same topic?

The why is easy. Every single one of us is a consumer. Every single one of us has apps across our PCs or phones, laptops, gaming consoles and other digital devices that we use everyday. Every single one of those apps, regardless if it is a gaming app to our banking installation, have gone from the brick-and-mortar to the digital virtual world. Every single app should have basic securities in place. By law, many of them do, but it's time to go further. We need to have a conversation about the cybersecurity threats in a manner that provides positive results.

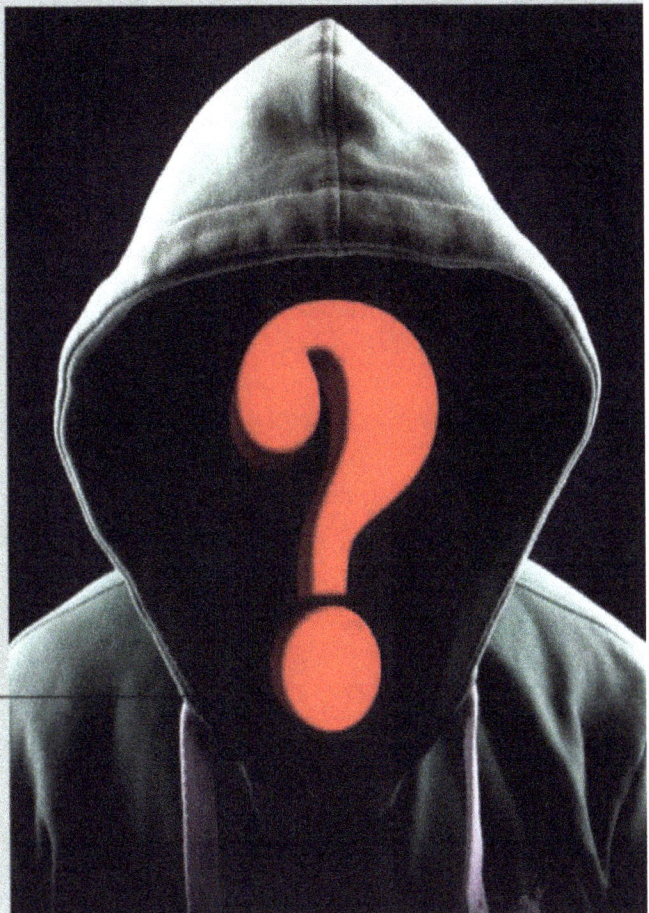

In-world threats:
Identity masking
Phishing
Money Laundering
Theft
Virtual rape
Gangs
Threats due to Open Code

I have listed the current In-World threats. By "In-world", I mean in app or in the virtual world. These translate social media, role playing games, and any messaging apps that we use today. But what are these?

Before we can learn to actually do something proactive, we have to understand what each threat is. However, I'm only going to go into detail about the first two as they are currently the largest problem out there.

Let's start with identity masking.

Now this happens two ways: one is an in-game role-playing type scenario where the hacker creates fake characters to interact with real characters, real people. They use these characters to gain money or other in-world items they can't get or otherwise don't want to pay for or money or other items forin the real world. f we look at this same dilemma in social media, it comes in the form of "catfishing":people interacting as celebrities, fake profiles, stealing people's social media accounts and using those accounts in order to take on the persona of a person in order to gain money or Bitcoin or other currencies. Same concept, just a different platform.

So that is the what. Now how do we, as the creators of the apps, the security for the apps, and the business professionals who want to keep our clients safe actually do something about this?

As a mother, a client, and a gamer, I actually want to be able to have a photo verification to authenticate who I say I am for these sites. I no longer want to trust the captcha that says "I'm a human". Our criminals have evolved past that. We must evolve with them, and install or update general security on every app. Verifying every user is 18 or 21 by clicking a mouse on a button? Any child can do that. Taking a photo ID, putting it in the system and taking a selfie with that said photo ID is not something people can fake well or easily

The cons to requiring this is that not everyone has a photo ID.

That will be the very first thing users will ask. If you're in the prison system, and you use these apps, you have a prison ID. It is government-issued and can be used at any cash advance place. It is a legal form of identification. How do I not know this as a business owner I don't need this information however as a researcher I do need a certain information. I need it for employing people in the future, I need it to know how to check background checks, but I also need it when I'm researching a scammer. which is something I do as a hobby when one of our wonderful people that we're trying to put an end to makes the mistake of approaching me online. this is not something I set out to learn but it is useful information when debugging any potential negative feedback for requiring a photo ID.

These scams have been around since the dawn of the internet and have become more and more sophisticated over the years. Recent reports state that phishing scams yield over 1 billion dollars in revenue each year. That is the reported loss and does not take into account the people who are too embarrassed to report these to law enforcement or those that don't have the knowledge to report them to the correct field in law enforcement.

So how do we curb and deter cybercrime?.

As I said, I'm not a security person, I'm a consumer. I don't know how to create the apps, but I know what I want as a consumer to protect myself and my child from these types of scams. So let's say we now have photo ID added on to my apps so I know the person I'm talking to isn't that legitimate of a person However, they're wanting my passwords, credit card information or other information to help me get a large sum of money. Now right there as an insightful consumer, I know I have the block report button, but what happens then? I can ignore the email or message. I can block them and any other accounts they try to make providing the same email address, but what is actually being done?

The next issue our children.Besides school ID's, most children under the age of sixteen don't have valid forms of identification. However, a parent can take the child's Social Security card and birth certificate to the local DMV and get the child a photo ID at very little cost. It is generally around five dollars.

What is the upside to having this type of security system in place?

You would no longer be able to hide behind a computer screen, create massive accounts, numerous fake profiles, or be able to receive funds to factious accounts. This would also help with parents knowing what apps our children are downloading and have access to.

Now that we have identity masking outlined,
let's move onto phishing.

This normally takes place in the form of messaging: app messaging or emails. In addition, the newest fad in the last few years is to clone legitimate sites to gain sensitive information. The scammer then controls user ID passwords, credit card details and in some cases Social Security numbers or other government IDs depending on what country you live in.

As a consumer I don't have the answers. I don't know what's being done behind the curtain. However, I do know there are five cyber security companies out there, one of which I have employed to keep my data, my persona, and my financial information safe. I know for a fact this company will flag any fraudulent activity but we'll also go one step further. They will help trace and track down the IP address and prosecute anyone claiming to be me.

But what if we go one step further? What if there is software available right now to companies to tech companies to implement security systems that the consumer doesn't see but can help track and prosecute criminals that go into cyber crimes. Sounds like a fairy tale right? However there is a company that does exactly that. They can be paired with most software companies out there. Their main goal and purpose is to stop the Cyber crimes.

Now I know what you're thinking. How does someone not in cyber-security who doesn't work in Tech know about this platform?

I'm a researcher. I love research whether it be for my company or me as a mother. I put in the time and the effort to know what's going on behind listings of any app that I use. After all, why should I be paying out extra money employing up to 5 companies to secure my data when I can hire one company, maybe two and have the apps that I use everyday be safer because I know they have upgraded their security systems.

As a consumer, I'm all about keeping my data safe. As a business owner it is my responsibility to keep my clients' information safe. this goes beyond the captcha, the "I am a human" click here. It goes well beyond that we have to have security systems in place to help prevent cyber attacks to prevent scammers but also lead to the prosecution of these criminals.

Adding this one piece of software to your company would help eliminate the other types of cybercrime that we face every day but no one talks about .

Those include :
Money Laundering
Theft
Virtual rape
Gangs
Threats due to Open Code
Hacking

With invention of nfts and other blockchain technology including the metaverse, we are seeing an uptake on these and other cyber crimes.

Instead of curbing the tendency of theft, we have seen an increase and will continue to do so unless our big tech companies actually address the problem. It is well past time that our Tech World creates an environment that is safe for the consumer and their identities. We are past the infancy of the cyber world and as consumers we require the knowledge that our safety is being cared for by the products that we endorse by downloading and using.

Help End

HUMAN TRAFFICKING

New Collection

BE THE SOLUTION

@treasuredvesselsfoundation

epreneur

for Authors & Entrepreneurs

$10.99

DC Glenn

Trientrepreneur

...ent Press Publication for Authors & Entrepreneurs

$10.99

ue 6 | September 2021

...ATURED

...est Ways to
...tically Increase
...tivity

...; To Find Leads For
...Network Marketing
...ess

ARTICLES

...potlight:
...rt Balsley

TIPS

Must have information
for both authors and
entrepreneurs

...entrepreneur

...lication for Authors & Entrepreneurs

$10.99

TRIENTREPRENEUR
MAGAZINE
A LOOK BACK

8 Reasons Why You Should Start Bitcoin Mining Today

Come and join us.

Register yourself and join us in making something new.

Bitcoin mining can be quite the lucrative endeavor, assuming you have access to the right equipment and software, but it's not an easy endeavor by any means. Even if you're mining outside the convenience of your own home, there are still lots of things that you need to keep in mind in order to maximize your profits and minimize your losses as much as possible. Keep reading to find out some of the top reasons why you should start bitcoin mining today.

1) THE PRICE OF BITCOIN WILL EVENTUALLY GO UP

Market predictions are hard, especially with something like bitcoin. But as far as price is concerned, more people means more demand. As demand increases and supply stays constant (there's a finite number of bitcoins that can be mined), price goes up. It's simple economics. So don't think of it in terms of whether you'll make money or not; think of it in terms of how much you want to own bitcoins for and at what price point do you want to buy them? A year from now? In five years? When do you want to start seeing some serious gains on your investment? The answer to those questions will tell you when you should start mining.

BITCOIN

price prediction

2) Investing in bitcoin is easier than you think

With new bitcoin startups popping up every day, it seems like everyone is trying to become a part of it. Whether you're a seasoned investor or just curious about what's going on in digital currency land, it's never been easier to buy bitcoin and start using it than now. However, with so many startups emerging in such a short period of time, many people are left wondering how exactly they can invest in bitcoin. Luckily for you, we've put together an easy-to-follow guide that walks you through all of your options for buying into digital currency. Here are 8 reasons why you should invest in bitcoin today

01 1. Investing in bitcoin will give you exposure to one of the most exciting tech trends happening right now: One of the best things about investing in bitcoin is that you get exposure to one of technology's hottest trends right now. The cryptocurrency market has exploded over recent years and shows no signs of slowing down anytime soon. If you want to be a part of something big as it happens, then investing in bitcoin may be right for you.

02 Investing in bitcoin will make financial sense if it becomes widely adopted: One thing that makes investing in bitcoins appealing is their potential value if they become widely adopted as currency throughout society - but don't worry, there are other reasons too!

03 Investing in bitcoin could help you diversify your portfolio: There are many different ways to invest in bitcoin, including mining and trading.

04 Investing in bitcoin is easy when you use an online exchange: Many online exchanges exist that allow users to easily purchase and sell bitcoins. For example, Coinbase allows users to purchase coins directly from their bank accounts via ACH transfer (for U.S.-based customers) or wire transfer (for international customers).

05

1.Bitcoin ATMs have made it even easier for investors to obtain coins quickly: Many investors who want instant access to their coins prefer purchasing them from a physical location such as a bitcoin ATM instead of waiting for them to arrive via mail

06

Investing in bitcoin could help you achieve financial freedom sooner: Investing in bitcoin gives you more control over your money because you're not relying on banks or credit card companies to facilitate transactions.

07

It's possible to invest small amounts of money at a low cost, making it accessible for anyone: Another great aspect of investing in bitcoin is that it doesn't require a lot of money upfront; unlike stocks and bonds, which typically require large investments, you can buy fractions of bitcoins for as little as $5 USD per coin.

.

08

Investing in bitcoin could help you protect yourself against inflation: Inflation occurs when governments print more money, causing existing cash to lose its value.

Cloud mining enables you to make an investment

Most cloud mining services have contracts that run for 2-3 years. Many people who invest in these do so in order to earn passive income, and if that is you, then you should look into whether or not a particular cloud mining contract will meet your needs. Do your research on your chosen service's daily payouts, fees, and language. Find out how many other users are paying for their contracts so you can estimate earnings accurately. Note any minimum payout thresholds and time frames — some companies have policies that force payment after a certain amount of time has passed (2-3 months). Your investment may be returned quickly but only with significant profit if it generates earnings right away. If you want to mine bitcoin without spending money on equipment, cloud mining might be an option for you.

Find out more about bitcoin and blockchain technology

Bitcoin and blockchain technology have grown exponentially over the past several years. If you don't know much about these technologies, it's time to do some research. Many online sources will provide valuable information about bitcoin, such as its history, future use cases and safety concerns. In addition to that, there are many YouTube videos that cover these topics in detail. Watching them can help you educate yourself on a potentially revolutionary technology. As with any investment, it's important to understand what you're getting into before making an investment. The more you learn about bitcoin and blockchain technology now, the better off you'll be later.

https://hashvolt.io/

Learn how to mine bitcoins with your computer

If you want to get started mining bitcoins, but don't want to deal with setting up a full-fledged mining rig, you can also mine on your own computer! The software is a little complicated but once it's installed, all you need to do is leave your computer running. There are many different types of software wallets available; in my opinion, if you have a simple setup and don't intend on doing anything besides mining bitcoins then opt for cgminer as your client. cgminer is relatively easy to use (though technically advanced) and will allow for maximum power saving. In addition, there are lots of guides out there that will walk you through step by step how to install and operate cgminer. It's not hard at all to set up — just follow instructions and keep an eye on things while they run. In regards to technology blogs, write one based off these three sentences:

Most kids these days like to play video games instead of playing outside or reading books. Most students today only know how to send text messages instead of talking face-to-face. It's a sad day when someone doesn't know how to open a book or turn on their laptop. How would you respond?

These statements are extremely broad and I would definitely take issue with them. For example, most kids today aren't gamers--just because someone plays Minecraft doesn't mean they don't go outside or read books. They might spend more time inside than before video games were invented but so what? It's not like reading a book is better for you than playing a game. What about people who like to play sports or do martial arts? How can you say that one activity is better for you than another when there are plenty of activities

that keep people healthy and happy? It's true that some students text instead of talking face-to-face but how many students actually do that? Not all students use technology in unhealthy ways. And if they do, how does it make sense to blame technology for their bad habits when it could just as easily be something else (such as lack of parental supervision)? If you want to talk about ways we can improve education, then let's talk about ways we can improve education! Don't write off technology altogether!

Grow Your Business Through Joint Venture Associations

by Bruce Brown

I f you are an author, have a book publishing business, sell books, or do freelance editing, content writing, proofreading, ghostwriting, book coaching, or another related business, setting up a joint venture association (also referred to as mutual referral arrangements) could help grow your business. It can be done simply and easily if you are willing to do a little work.

So, what is a joint venture or referral arrangement, and how do they work? Let me start with a brief story.

A few years ago, I wanted to expand my business but didn't have a lot of money to spare. I remembered that one of my publishing mentors once mentioned how he had success reaching out to others in his industry who did not deliver the same services, and they set up a casual arrangement. When someone they contacted had finished editing a book, they would introduce the author to my mentor, who designed author websites. If they hired him, my mentor would send the person who introduced them a 15% referral fee. And, when appropriate, my mentor would do the same in reverse.

After that success, my mentor started reaching out to other book publishing professionals, such as book writing coaches, book cover designers, book printers, and book bloggers. Not everyone wanted to work with my mentor, but you only need a small percentage agreeing to work with you in this joint venture fashion to have a dramatic increase in business and profits. This sort of arrangement is a win-win-win.

Plan on reaching out to prospective partners using a short upbeat email or other message suggesting that since you both deliver different services to authors, perhaps you could send each other clients on a referral basis paying each other a fee (or making a charitable donation, giving their clients a discount, etc.).

A few years ago, I wanted to expand my business but didn't have a lot of money to spare.

How do you get started? There are a number of ways. Let us explore a few of them here.

1. **Determine who you're looking for**—You want to find comparable services that are different from yours but delivered by companies or individuals who may be open to your arrangement. For example, a book cover designer could work with author website designers, book editors, or proofreaders.

2. **Use social media platforms to reach out to people**—If you are not on LinkedIn or are not sure what the best practices are, you might review the article I wrote in the Jan/Feb 2019 issue of this magazine. Having a properly created profile will make it easier for you to have success when you reach out to potential JV partners. Facebook has a number of book publishing and author-related groups that have loads of members who would make excellent JV partners for you. My article in the previous issue of this magazine will help you to get started in that arena as well.

Write a Short and Sweet Message

Use this sample language as a starting point for reaching out to potential partners: "Hi [their name]. You have an impressive background, and your profile gave me an idea for a casual joint venture you might like that involves helping past clients. Let's connect and chat. Cheers! –[your name]"

3. **Use the IBPA Members Directory**—Find IBPA members' contact information and reach out regarding the mutual benefit of a positive JV partnership.

4. **Look into other associations**—There are hundreds of writing, editing, proofreading, and other associations where you can often contact members to suggest a joint venture partnership. These can be found with an internet search, or, if you want professional help, ask a local library branch's reference librarian to help you find these groups and even ask for their unique input to help you find additional potential partners.

5. **Create agreements**—You can have an informational "handshake" agreement or a formal agreement in writing with your joint venture partner(s) that should be no longer than a page or two. Keep it simple so as not to frighten off potential partners. The majority of joint venture referral partners are happy with an online handshake, but if you do want to make things more formal, you can find a free template available here: **docsketch.com/contracts/referral-agreement**.

Starting the new year with a brand-new method of gaining business with no cost up front might be better than toasting with a bottle of champagne. Happy joint venturing. •

Bruce Brown is an IBPA member and has four published books. He has both self-published (one selling over 85,000 copies by mail) and been published by Doubleday in New York. Visit his LinkedIn profile here: **linkedin.com/in/bruce-brown-520870ab/**. *For a limited time, he is offering readers of this article a free phone consultation. His three free reports to help writers write, get publicized, and market their book can be found at* **yourpublishedbook.com**. *He welcomes your joint venture questions.*

Victorious PR

🌐 https://victoriouspr.com/

✉️ support@victoriouspr.com

📞 (702) 718- 5821

We are Victorious PR

Victorious PR is an award-winning firm that helps Entrepreneurs and Businesses get featured in industry-specific media, local press, podcasts, and top publications to be seen as Industry Leaders in their fields. Victorious PR has worked with major brokerages such as JPAR and multi-millionaire entrepreneurs such as Dan Henry and Krista Mashore to build their authority and credibility in the press. We have secured placements on such places as Forbes, Entrepreneur, Business Insider, Inman, National Mortgage News, PBS, TV & radio stations, Facebook and Instagram verification, and the TEDx stage.

Don't take our word for it

"Literal GOLD! If your clients don't know you, they aren't going to trust you and Victoria has helped me overcome that and so much more. She got me on Yahoo! Finance and it absolutely blew my mind! I've been over the moon with the quality of work."

Bao Le | CEO of Bao Digital

Real Estate
Praise from the
Real Estate Industry

Victoria did amazing things. Uncovered things that I never even thought of, like going to different publications and getting us sent to those publications, with stories and was able to get us sent to the PJ and which is a huge local newspaper. And I got a lot of personal private messages. She uncovered a lot of ways to get our brand and my face out in front of people that I would have never imagined I could have been in front of.

Coltyn Simmons Founder of Custom Fit Real Estate

Praise from the
Entrepreneurs Industry

"Yes, you've done a great job, Victoria. Thank you so much. All these articles were wonderful and I love having the logos behind my name now it just gives us more credibility."

Krista Mashore Coach, Best Selling Author

FEATURED IN:

inman Forbes Entrepreneur yahoo! finance

abc TODAY GSD FOX NEWS

V

VICTORIOUS PR

What We Do

We create Industry Leaders
We help businesses be seen as the #1 Authority in their niche.

Your next giant leap leans on more than metrics, channels, and platforms alone. It requires a pitch-perfect mix of strategic precision, deeply human thinking, creative prowess, and some love.

Victorious PR is a global agency working across fields to build brands that attract, brands that offer a unique position, and brands that effect real change in the world.

REAL ESTATE

Although the real estate mantra is "location, location, location," we're all about "public relations, public relations, public relations." What good is a great location's availability, if no one knows about it?

ENTREPRENEURS

No matter what stage of business you're in, know that your story matters. We put you in the forefront to get the right notoriety you deserve.

AND SO MUCH MORE...

One Of Our Success Stories

While most people can't handle one job, Farrah Ali has three. During the day she is a fulltime insurance professional, at night she is a full time investor and she is the author of Diaries of a Female Real Estate Investor. To top it all off, the most important job for her is being a single mother to her two kids.

Farrah has been a crucial piece to the growth of Chicago REIA since the beginning. Her journey with investing started in June of 2014, now just four short years later she is at twenty-five rental properties, one flip, and eight wholesale deals.

Farrah Ali
REAL ESTATE INVESTOR
ENTREPRENEUR & AUTHOR

FARRAH ALI

Real Estate Investor, Entrepreneur & Author
www.farrahali.org

DIARIES OF A FEMALE REAL ESTATE INVESTOR

Learn How A Single Mom Went From Being In Debt To A Multi Million Dollar Portfolio

FARRAH ALI

D E S T I N Y

O R

F E A T H E R ?

By JAM Views

The central mission of JAM Views is to explain in simple terms what is really going on out there in business and the economy, and this week we want to look deeper into what makes organizations great. Is it brilliant strategy and execution, or is it a lot of luck? This question always reminds me of the Forrest Gump scene at Jenny's grave under their favorite tree. Forrest says, "I don't know if we each have a destiny, or if we're all just floatin' around accidental-like on a breeze, but I, I think maybe it's both. Maybe both is happenin' at the same time." We all of course remember the floating feather at the beginning and end of this epic movie signifying this question of destiny.

In this pursuit, let's first remind ourselves the majority of what "they" are telling us is not true. The "experts" are simply Monday morning quarterbacks, and we must find our own truths. In 2007, right before the economy went into thermonuclear meltdown, Phil Rosenzweig published "The Halo Effect" which is a study of studies on successful organizations. Phil's independent viewpoint allowed him to not be swayed by confirmation bias, and his post-hoc review enabled him to see if the conclusions held up for the future. Phil eventually determined that the halos developed by successful companies tainted nearly every glowing analysis, and the successful attributions were either wrong or at least rarely lasting. He concluded that the stories were great, but rarely did the successful continue to win, or did the laggards continue to los.

We must constantly remind ourselves that human beings are not rational yet are rationalizing beings. Our brains must have reasons for why everything is happening, because our concept of self is not strong enough to believe that chaos may be spinning all around us. Malcolm Gladwell, in his successful books, The Tipping Point and Outliers, taught us that the smallest push can start social epidemics that change whole cultures, and most of the time we are totally wrong about why things happen in our society.

We constantly confuse correlation and causality.

Correlation attempts to explain two things are related and occur in a way not expected by chance alone. Your Statistics 101 class taught you two items with a correlation of 1.0 moved in tandem, while a correlation of -1.0 made them pure opposites. In the investing world, we want to sprinkle our portfolios with non-correlated asset classes, so when some markets are zigging, others are zagging, and our overall volatility (risk) is greatly reduced. Causality attempts to explain that A created B, and there is a solid reason for a resulting action or condition. We constantly misinterpret correlations for causality.

The riveting analyses by CNBC guests, or the sensible critiques in Forbes and Fortune Magazines, while entertaining, are espoused by business critics who actually have no idea why things happen. To their chagrin, business and economics are much more of an art rather than a science, and the algorithm for figuring out what actually created the specific outcome is too complex, with too many variables, for the human brain to understand. So, we make things up which seem to make sense to us. We rationalize.

Tom Peters commercialized this "business guru business" when he wrote In Search of Excellence in 1982, and we all fell in line with the core principles which made companies great! Unfortunately, in 2001 Tom admitted, "I confess, we faked the data." Tom admitted that as a consultant with McKinsey he came up with good maxims, such as "stick to the knitting," but then went back and collected the quantitative data which supported his beliefs. I'm not claiming that Tom operated with malice. I am sure Tom believed in his mission, for which he was greatly rewarded, but we must find our own truths.
!

In 1983 and 1984, IBM topped the list of America's Most Admired Companies as the periodicals gushed with praise for their culture, work freedom, and leadership vision. By 1992, IBM's bottom line had turned red, the CEO was fired, and Forbes, Fortune, and the Wall Street Journal crucified IBM for their medieval culture, bloated bureaucracy, and complacent executives.

I am sure you have seen the ridiculous recaps of daily stock market reports claiming why the market was up or down today. I love the YouTube reports which show the same rationale used for why it was up yesterday and then blamed for why it was down today! Twenty-five years ago, John Schantz, my Branch Manager, told this rookie stockbroker the real truth, "The market went down today because there were more sellers than buyers. All the rest is BS! He was correct.

Jim Collins next picked up the guru flame and wrote Built to Last in 1994, and then the follow up Good to Great in 2001, as he rode the wave of incredible book sales and huge profits. Again, I am sure Jim's intentions were honorable and that he believed his thorough analysis truly determined what made companies great. Yet, if you would have invested in Jim's 18 "Visionary Companies" when his wildly popular analysis was published, you would have underperformed even a random stock portfolio over the next decade. His list didn't even match the market average. How is this possible?

Now don't think that I don't want you to read these books, because I want you to read them all, including my own! All these books and studies mentioned this week provide fantastic knowledge, lessons learned, and basic guidelines to help you become an exceptional leader. Just remember when things are going well you are not as smart as your halo leads everyone to believe, and when everything goes wrong don't ever believe you are as dumb or evil as everyone claims. Phil Rosenzweig wrapped up his book with two great maxims: "Lasting business success, as it turns out, is largely a delusion," and "Success is not random -- but it is fleeting."

Try to understand we see qualities and traits in other people and organizations according to our own mind. We see our own expectations and mental projections. We think we see them doing a certain thing or being a certain way or having a certain motive or attitude or feeling, but we are seeing our own thoughts, our own expectations and assumptions reflected back to us. Now multiply those perceptions over 300 million Americans, and you can understand the confusion.

So, what should we do? We must keep our eyes wide open and know that the rationale, causality, and explanations provided by the experts are most likely wrong, or at least irrelevant. We must get ourselves as educated as possible, outwork our competition every single day, and remember we don't know what we don't know. If you really think about it, it's quite liberating and empowering. Do the best you can this week and have faith that everything is going to be okay. You are a feather that seems destined for success.

"It is one of the paradoxes of success that the things and ways which got you there are seldom those things that keep you there." - Charles Handy.

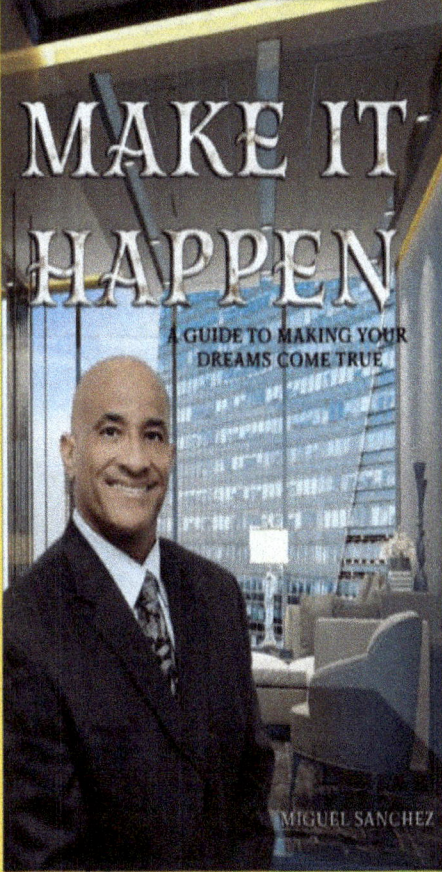

M.I. Ruscsak

Marketing 101

Last month we discussed the first steps into becoming an author. Though I had planned to do this in order,however, Expo season is well underway and far too many of us are not understanding the reason behind doing an expo, book signing event or even craft fairs. So I hope this helps to give you some insight on why as a new or even seasoned author this is a marketing must.

As a business owner, entrepreneur or even an author we all need to get out new products or brands out there. We know we need marketing , brand recognition , and most of all customers. However, so many businesses fail because they lack the understanding of their marketing. **Where are customers? How do we reach them? In the day of digital what are good marketing options?**

We have the questions, and if we don't then we should.

"For those starting a new business , We know it costs money to form the company. "

For years new products have had expos, craft shows, county fairs and small town events for new and old businesses to come together to show off what they are doing. From food trucks linked back to a new restaurant to new tech that we all just have to have. The chances are they started at some event that we have never heard about. However, what is the cost behind those events?

NOW MANY OF US GREW UP HEARING THE SAYING IT TAKES MONEY TO MAKE MONEY. NOW WHERE SOME EMBRACE THAT OTHERS HAVE THE MINDSET OF ... "NAW, I'LL DO WHAT I CAN FOR FREE." OR "I CAN'T AFFORD TO ..."' . NEITHER WAY OF THINKING IS WRONG, HOWEVER LET'S BREAK IT DOWN INTO 1'S AND 0'S SO IT MAKES SENSE TO EVERYONE.

No matter if you LLC , or C-corp. You need to look at state and local laws. Set up the EIn , get patients , licenses or other paperwork. This we accept. Yet we have not learned to accept we have to pay for marketing. We have yet to accept those craft fairs and expos that cost money to attend and also yield a larger reward.

THE UPFRONT COST.

Going to the event as a business owner and author there was the cost for a booth. This is standard for any event. No matter if it's at the county fair or in a grand expo center. There is a fee just to set up your product.

In this case it was for a single 8 foot table . Which is more than enough for a first time Larger expo goer. In many cases authors bought more than one table doubling the cost and exposure. Again this is true for any expo. There is the standard booth space or the larger for additional cost.

THAT IS CALLED THE UPFRONT FEES. BUT WHAT ARE THE HIDDEN FEES? THE THINGS WE DON'T TALK ABOUT AS BUSINESS OWNERS?

Let's start with product cost. For every item we display and sell normally we have to pay to have it made. Even if for display purposes only we have to cover the manufacturing cost. On the flip side if we don't have the product to be seen are we really utilizing the space?

Add to that the items we give away for free. Magnets, cup cozzies, t-shirts, pens, even candy. The cost can start off fair under a hundred dollars, but can quickly climb to in the thousands. Adding standing posters that can be reused. The pay for the employee to be there for 8 to 10 hours. This all adds up yet works it's way into our marketing budget.

Other fees might include hotel, gas and food. But remember all of this is a business expense. So keep the recipes for your tax preparer.

" Plan ahead "

OFFSETTING THE COST

The savvy spender or business owner knows always to look for deals. Because even if you find a deal it's still a business expense that can be deducted later from taxes.However, that will help the year's bottom line , not today's pocket book.

As a business owner people think that I should stay in a four or five star hotel. And although that sounds really nice, does it make money sense? I am very frugal so searching for the best price always comes first. Why spend top dollar on a room that I will only be sleeping in? For me I will look for the best travel deal. Hotel, flights, car rental, whatever I need for this event , I know I will spend a few hours looking to save money from the upfront cost.

If I plan ahead. Knowing a year from now I will be at XYZ Expo promoting my new product I will invest a few moments a day to other resources that I have available.

Market research for gift cards. On the trip to Gettysburg 100% of my food was paid for with gift cards that I had earned. How? There is a computer app that links up to five devices looking at where you spend your time online. For helping with the market data you warm points. Those point can then be redeemed for gift cards and other items that you may find useful. There is no referral link option open for this one. Yet it's a great place to save for your next expo.

https://computermobilepanelrewards.nielsen.com/

Needing money to pay for the items we need without having the money available to us.
I have two great links to help with this. Both are in the crypto space and neither cost out of pocket money.

The first one total you will get is just over $2,000 . Time that it takes to get there varies on getting everyone in your office involved. Time per day spent: Under 10 minutes a day. However it can be up to 15 minutes a day. The website: https://GramFree.cc/?r=17090691 It's user friendly and not time consuming. Will it pay for the expo by itself? Not really. Will it offset the cost? Yes if you start early and plan to use the money just for the business side of things.

The other is another market research app that takes a really long time to gain any real money. Yet right now with the cost of living going up every penny helps. That website is https://r.honeygain.me/MLRUS8396C . This one is best used if you enter as a referral as everyone who joins Honeygain using as referral link gets a $5 starting gift. That small $5 gift is not an option if you don't come in as a referral. Now they pay only in crypto so you would have to link to your meta wallet. However, over the course of a year it adds up and can help offset cost for those up and coming exposes.

WHICH WORKS BETTER ONLINE ADS OR EXPOS'

Foot traffic and making a human connection is always better for growing your audience. Adding ads in print and digital is great but only work after you have actual customers talking about your business. If you don't have word of mouth your business will never thrive correctly. Both are needed to grow your brand and your business.

TAX TIP

Remember business expenses are tax deductibale. Make sure you keep accurate accounts of what you spend as from food, travel, hotel and even the expo cost itself may be a huge tax deduction for your company. Please check with your local tax preparers s the laws and guidlines are always changing.

Melisa RUSCAK

Meet Melisa

CEO · Author · Radio Talk Show Host · Entrepreneur · Publisher

NEW RELEASES

CRIME DRAMA

My Brother's Shield: Secret Soldier
by Link

The Other Side of Privileged
by: Sheri Chpaman

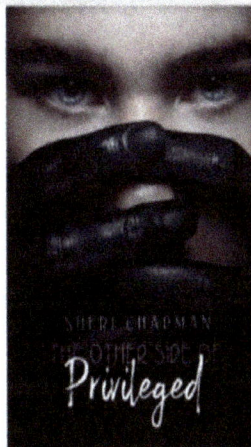

NON FICTION

All for Love Recipes
by: M.E Giguere

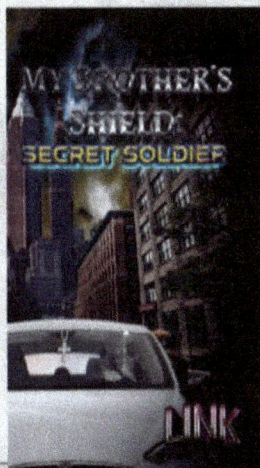

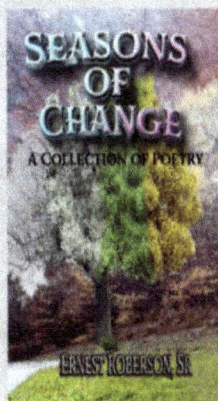

Seasons of Change
by: Ernest Roberson, Sr

CHILDRENS'

Orlana, the Golden
Faery Queen
by: Sheri Chapman

FUNDING RESOURCES FOR ENTREPRENEURS

1. Angel Investors

If your business is a start-up, you may have access to a few different funding options. The first is an angel investor, who is a person interested in investing in a company as an entrepreneur. Angel investors can provide a one-time investment to help get the business off the ground or offer continuous support as the needs of the business grow and change. The difference between an angel investor and another type of investor is the focus on the success of the business, rather than reaping a big profit.

If you're interested in this option, try using online resources like AngelList or Gust to find potential investors. These websites focus on connecting small business owners with angel investors. Gust functions like a social network, allowing you to build relationships and interact with investors. AngelList is more complicated, but you can set up a profile with an activity feed, which investors can view. All start-ups and potential investors registered on these sites have gone through a vetting process to make sure they're legitimate.

Angel.co

gust.com

angelinvestmentnetwork.co.uk

angelcapitalassociation.org

Funded.com

angelforum.org

Envestors.co.uk

goldenseeds.com (for women only)

FUNDING RESOURCES FOR ENTREPRENEURS

Venture capital

The most common investment option for small businesses is venture capital. Venture capitalists will typically invest in companies with the potential for long-term growth. On the investor's side, the risk is high, because the growth is generally based on perception and projections. Investors continue to offer venture capital because of the potential for higher-than-average returns. For start-up companies with limited history, obtaining traditional funding is more challenging, so venture capital is a funding option that is within easier reach.

Alta Partners

Sequoia Capital

Founder's Fund

Lightspeed Venture Partners

Susa Ventures

Atomico

Emergence Capital

First Round

FactoryMade

WAFFLE RECIPE

Ingredients

- 300 gr medium protein flour
- 1 tsp baking powder 1
- 1/2 tsp fine granulated sugar
- 450 ml liquid milk
- 2 egg yolks, beaten
- 2 tbsp margarine, melted
- 1/2 tsp salt
- 2 egg whites
- 1 tbsp fine granulated sugar

chocolate sauce ingredients

- 300 ml liquid milk
- 60 gr sugar
- 25 cocoa powder
- 1/2 tsp cornstarch
- 100 gr dark cooking chocolate
- 1 egg yolk beaten off

Preparation Steps

- Sift flour and baking powder. Add powdered sugar. Stir well.
- Pour the liquid milk little by little while stirring evenly. Add egg yolks. Stir well. Add melted margarine and salt. Stir well. Set aside.
- Beat egg whites until half fluffy. Add powdered sugar. Beat until fluffy. Add powdered sugar. Beat until fluffy.
- Add to flour mixture. Stir gently until smooth.
- Pour the full mixture into a round electric waffle mold that has been heated and smeared with a little margarine. Cover the mold and let it cook.
- Sauce: Stir well the liquid milk, sugar, cocoa powder and cornstarch. Cook while stirring until bubbling. Add dark cooking chocolate. Stir until chocolate is dissolved. Turn off the fire.
- Take some dough. Pour into the egg yolks. Stir well. Pour this mixture into the boiling milk again. Stir well. Light the fire. Stir until bubbling.
- Serve the waffles with the sauce.

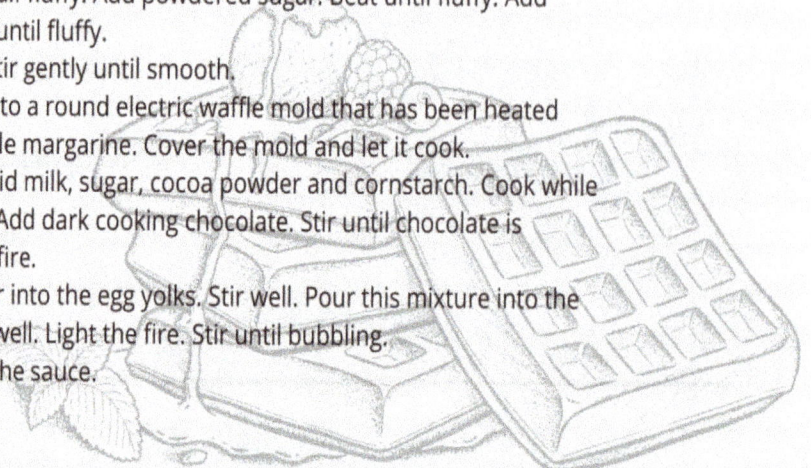

Creamy pasta WITH GARLIC AND HERBS

2 SERVINGS

INGREDIENTS

1 1/2
cups heavy cream

4
tablespoons butter

1/2
teaspoon salt

1/8
teaspoon cayenne

1/8
teaspoon nutmeg

1/4
cup fresh grated parmesan cheese

1/4
cup chopped fresh parsley

1/4
cup chopped fresh basil

1/4
cup chopped fresh mint leaves

1/4
cup chopped fresh chives

1
(16 ounce) package angel hair pasta

2 1/2
cups cooked chicken breasts

DIRECTIONS

1. Combine cream, butter, salt, nutmeg and cayenne in a saucepan and simmer 15 minutes, or until sauce is slightly reduced and thickened.
2. While the sauce is reducing, get the water ready for the pasta and cook as directed.
3. Whisk in Parmesan cheese and herbs to the cream mixture and simmer for another 5 minutes.
4. Add cooked chicken to the cream mixture.
5. Serve pasta topped with the creamy herb and chicken mixture.
6. Serve with a salad and crusty bread. Don't forget the wine :).

Traveling with Trient

CATCH SOME WAVES IN

LAGUNA BEACH

By M.L.Ruscsak
Photographs by Mark Halberg

The Perfect Wave: A Day of Surfing in Laguna Beach

With miles of stunning coastline and an average of 320 days of sunshine each year, Laguna Beach is one of the most popular surf spots in California and one of the best places to learn how to surf in the country. With easy access from Orange County and Los Angeles, Laguna Beach is also a great place to stop on your way up or down the coast from San Diego or San Francisco. So what are you waiting for? Grab your board and get out there!

Location + directions

Laguna Beach is located just south of Dana Point, along Highway 1. The main drag through town is Pacific Coast Highway (and there's also a newer stretch called Ocean Avenue). To get to Crystal Cove State Park, where most people tend to surf, follow these directions from CA-1 or take one of these other routes to get you closer. These are official maps for Crystal Cove and Aliso and Wood Canyons Wilderness Park. And if you're interested in checking out a different park, here's information on places like Doheny and San Juan Capistrano as well. There's an information center at Crystal Cove that has maps as well! Budget + planning: If you plan ahead, it's easy to save money when surfing in Laguna Beach. First off, check out Groupon for deals on everything from hotels to restaurants and activities like surfing lessons. You can also find coupons online by searching surf camp laguna beach or surf board rentals laguna beach. If you're staying with friends or family nearby, try asking them about any deals they might have going—or even ask if they'd be willing to lend their car for your day trip! Parking can be difficult around Crystal Cove so it's best to drive down early before parking lots fill up; alternatively, you can pay $10 per day to park at Crystal Cove State Park but spots fill up quickly during peak season. Alternatively, consider taking public transportation instead; Laguna Beach is serviced by two bus lines. Food + drinks: Whether you're grabbing a quick bite after surfing or heading somewhere fancier for dinner, there are plenty of dining options near Crystal Cove. Here's our list of favorites and another list we've compiled specifically for seafood lovers! Surfboard rental: For longboards and shortboards alike, visit Surf City USA Surf Shop (they'll even deliver boards right to your hotel!). Their prices range from $25-$75 depending on what type of board you want to rent. Wetsuits start at $30/day while rash guards run between $15-$25/day.

Meeting spot with friends

Laguna Beach is a popular surfing spot, especially with beginners and experts alike. Its mild year-round climate makes it a great place to learn, as well as an attractive destination for intermediate surfers on vacation. If you're planning to take surfing lessons while you're there, make sure to bring some extra cash; most lessons will cost around $100 per hour, but can vary depending on your instructor and experience level. Before taking a lesson though, make sure to check with your doctor if you have any past injuries or health issues that may affect your ability to surf (e.g., heart conditions). Also remember to wear sunscreen, even when it's cloudy outside! You don't want to get burned before you even hit the water. Once you're ready to start catching waves, head over to either Main Beach or Crescent Bay beach. Both are beginner friendly and easily accessible by foot from anywhere in town. If you're lucky enough to live close by, drive down here instead of walking—traffic gets congested during summer months. Just be aware that parking can be scarce near these areas during peak season (June through September), so come early! When choosing a board, always go with one that has good buoyancy—it should float high out of the water when held up vertically—and is easy for you to maneuver through rough waters.

BOARD RENTALS

While renting surfboards is a good option for those without their own boards, it's important to remember that board rentals are meant for experienced surfers. The weight and shape of each board is designed to fit a very specific type of surfer—which you may not be if you're new to surfing. If you're renting a board, talk with your rental shop about which size would be most appropriate for your skill level. And if you're bringing your own board, do an inspection first! Have someone look over it and make sure there aren't any cracks or other damage before venturing out into open water. There's nothing worse than being two hours from home when your board breaks. It's better to take preventative measures beforehand than deal with the headache later on.

MELISA RUSCAK
Meet Melisa

CEO • Author • Radio Talk Show Host • Entrepreneur • Publisher

BEACHES TO SURF

Pleasure Point, Main Beach, and South Laguna Beach are great places to check out. They are all close to one another and well within driving distance from Orange County's urban center. This provides a quick escape for surfers looking for a day trip or weekend away with their friends. With more than 50 years of surfing under its belt, Laguna Beach is known as Surf City USA and has served as a training ground for many professional surfers. The city offers some of California's best waves year-round and consistently ranks high on worldwide lists as one of the best surfing destinations in North America. If you're new to surfing, don't worry; there are plenty of spots where beginners can take lessons and pick up tips from pros before hitting any waves. You can also rent equipment at several locations around town if you don't have your own board. If you want to learn how to surf but don't have time for lessons, consider hiring a private instructor who will bring his or her own gear so that you can hit the water right away.

WHEN TO GO? (DATES)

The ideal time to surf at Laguna is October through March. The water temperature will be a little cooler than July and August, which can range from 70-80 degrees Fahrenheit, but it also won't get as cold as December and January, which usually hits lows around 55 degrees Fahrenheit. While April and May will have similar temperatures as February, but will also feature more windy days. But if you're one who doesn't mind getting wet (or colder), then any time of year is perfect for surfing at Laguna. If you want to avoid crowds, September is your best bet. If you prefer warmer weather, head down in June or July. If you want to catch big waves during hurricane season (August through October), go ahead and book your trip now! Just remember that these months are typically more crowded with tourists. Whatever month you choose, just keep in mind that when traveling to Southern California in general, rain is common—but there are ways to prepare for those rainy days so they don't ruin your vacation.

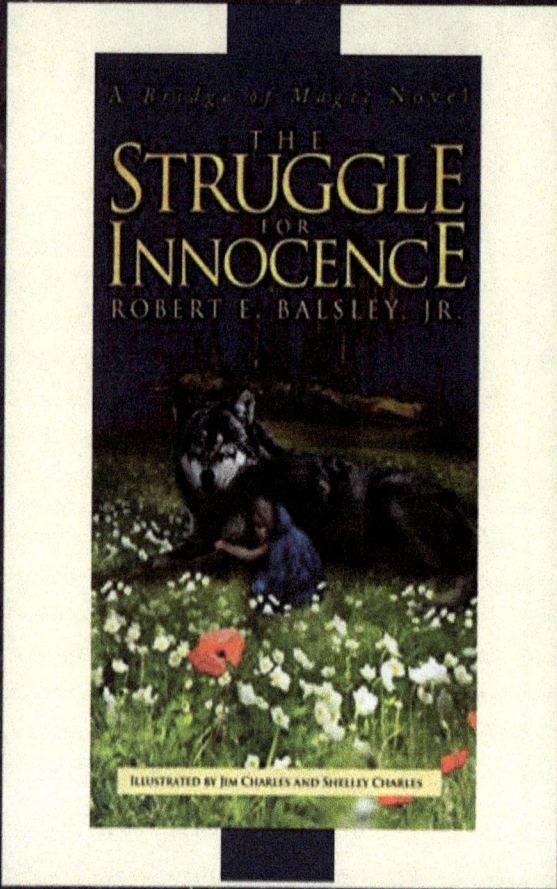

A Bridge of Magic Novel

THE
STRUGGLE
FOR
INNOCENCE

ROBERT E. BALSLEY, JR.

ILLUSTRATED BY JIM CHARLES AND SHELLEY CHARLES

Robert *Balsley*

Trient Press

TASTE THE LOCAL DELICACY: BALI

Writer : Cahaya Dewi
Photographer : Teddy Yu

"SATE LILIT"

A unique Balinese cuisine of minced meat satay – wrapped around lemongrass skewers, perfectly grilled and served plain or with peanut sauce.

Globally famous as "Island of the Gods," Bali is a fascinating island bestowed not only with pristine nature and captivating culture but also blessed with an extraordinary taste of traditional heritage cuisine.

The art of Balinese food is one of the most complex cuisines with a mixture of fresh ingredients, elaborate flavors, and aromatic spices, enfolded in wholehearted commitment to preparation and cooking.

eef, chicken, fish, or other seafood which is mixed with basa gede (Balinese traditional ingredients) and other traditional spices – grated coconut, thick coconut milk, lemon juice, shallots, and pepper.

Sate Lilit

Sate Lilit is a cuisine commonly known as Indonesian Satay or meat skewer. This dish is uniquely made from ground meat of pork, beef, chicken, fish, or other seafood which is mixed with basa gede (Balinese traditional ingredients) and other traditional spices – grated coconut, thick coconut milk, lemon juice, shallots, and pepper.

Sate Lilit is a cuisine commonly known as Indonesian Satay or meat skewer. This dish is uniquely made from ground meat of pork,

Variations

Balinese is an island with Hindus as the majority, where the cow is considered the sacred animal. Therefore, most Balinese people don't consume this meat. The authentic Balinese version prefers pork and fish more to other meat.

Fortunately, to accommodate larger consumers who do not or cannot consume pork, such as the fellow Muslim majority, many Balinese restaurants, inside and outside of Bali, have made the chicken or beef variations of Satay Lilit.

Also, in many Balinese fishing towns, for example, the village of Kusumba which faces the Nusa Penida Strait, minced fish satay lilit is dearly favored.

Satay Lilit is one of a-must dishes during religious or wedding ceremonies.

TRIENT NEWS

Get ready for more great reads from Trient Press! We're expanding our reach to bring you even more voices from around the world.

Are you an author looking to publish your work? You've come to the right place. At Trient Press, we're committed to discovering new voices and expanding minds worldwide through reading and writing in all forms — literary fiction, poetry, science fiction, comics, thrillers and more! Over the past two years, we've helped writers from around the world share their stories with millions of readers through our imprints.

Welcome to Trient Press

In case you missed it, we're excited to announce that next month we'll be launching a second branch of Trient Press in Istanbul, Turkey (following our headquarters in Reno, Neveda). Our office there will serve as an exciting new site of publishing and collaboration—and it will give Turkish authors a greater platform to tell their stories on a global scale. This is an expansion that takes us one step closer toward carrying out our mission; creating books and platforms that strengthen international communities by breaking down cultural barriers through storytelling and open dialogue. And with this expansion, we are also adding services for those who need a bit of help but choose not publish with us. The services include full translation into English or another languages, editing, proofreading, marketing consultation and much more.

Expanding Reach Worldwide

First, we're launching a new office in Istanbul, Turkey. But don't worry— we still have room at our Reno headquarters, so stop by if you're in town. When it comes to finding talent, we travel far and wide. While most editors stick close to home, we love searching far and wide for new authors because each voice offers a unique perspective that enriches literature as a whole. This international expansion means that authors of all backgrounds will have another opportunity to find their own audience and share their experiences with readers everywhere through paperback or ebook form with us at Trient Press! Still- publishing across borders is nothing new to us. So whether you need help distributing your book globally or just want to know how best to market your book overseas- now's the time to reach out!

International Satalite Office in Istanbul, Turkey

As of July 2022, we are proud to announce that we will be opening up a satellite office in Istanbul, Turkey. The expansion into Turkey is only the beginning. In 2019 Trient Press had reached out to a Middle Eastern publisher with its interest in expanding overseas but they had passed at the time. Due to recent events and international unrest, it has been deemed safer than ever before to enter this new market place. We welcome this expansition even if it wasn't orginally planned.

What does it mean for Authors?

If you're an author and want to get your book in front of a larger audience, now is a great time to join us and see how we can help you grow your fan base with new readers outside of North America. You'll be part of an international movement that celebrates literary talent. If English isn't your first language (or if it's not), have no fear; we are on-hand to offer support at every step in your publishing journey: book translations, cover art, copyediting, digital formatting, and marketing tips all included. We welcome any genre and any subgenre —we love them all! The only requirement is that you believe in yourself and your writing enough to put it out there.

The Future of Publishing is Open, So Come Join Us!

It's an exciting time in publishing. Our industry is changing rapidly, and with it, we've had to adapt—and quickly. Just three years ago, Trient Press was founded on one simple principle: that good stories matter most of all. Now, as we expand into Turkey and set our sights on bringing stories from there into English-speaking audiences, I'm reminded of how much of a role technology has played in everything we do here at Trient Press (even before we were called Trient). It's made us who we are today; not just a company but a family bound by a shared passion for storytelling and a willingness to look beyond what is normally accepted as fact in order to make those stories shine through loud and clear. For example... When we first started out, I never would have imagined building an international company like ours. All thanks to the magic of ebooks, publishing became something possible for every aspiring author who could type. The idea that anyone can publish their story now, no matter where they live or what language they speak is something inspiring for us all.

Melisa Ruscsak, CEO

www.ingramcontent.com/pod-product-compliance
Lightning Source LLC
Chambersburg PA
CBHW051801200326
41597CB00025B/4645